Money MAGIC

Jon Day

Illustrated by

Chris Fisher

Contents

Kingfisher Books

All about money magic

This book shows you how to do thirteen great tricks with coins. On these pages you can find some tips and hints to help you become a successful magician.

You don't have to dress up to do tricks, but it's fun to wear a **cloak** and **hat** for special performances, and they may help you give a particularly brilliant performance!

Remember, **pockets** are very important pieces of equipment. Make sure your performing outfit has good-sized, easily reached pockets.

Some tricks require **special equipment** such as sticky tape, scissors, elastic bands etc. Where these things are needed, they are listed at the beginning of each trick.

The most important thing you need is **practice.** Try tricks out over and over again in private until you can do them easily and smoothly.

Tricks are usually described and illustrated from the right-handed person's point of view. If you are left-handed just reverse the instructions. Perform tricks in whatever way feels most comfortable for you.

Tricks with money are fun to do. As you learn how to do the tricks in this book, you will find out how to make money vanish, change in value or even multiply itself! Everyone is interested in money, so it should be easy to hold your audience's attention.

Try tricks out in front of a mirror so you can get an 'audience's eye view'.

Coins are not usually very clean, so don't put them near your mouth. Wash your hands after handling coins.

One special piece of equipment is a **coin chute.** You can learn how to make one on page 24.

Hints

1 Money tricks are most effective if you borrow the coins from your audience, rather than use your own. That way everyone will know you have not used special trick coins, and they will be even more impressed by your magic skills.

2 Make sure you have all the equipment ready and in the right place before you start to do a trick.

3 Keep your secrets secret! Don't show people how tricks work. And don't repeat tricks straight away, as someone may realize how the trick is done.

The drop flip

Things you need

Any coin

Drop a coin on the floor, and make it vanish into thin air!

Trick time

This simple trick is surprisingly convincing when done well.

1 Show the coin to your audience. As you do so, pretend to be clumsy and drop the coin on the floor near your foot.

2 While everyone laughs at you, bend down to pick up the coin, apologizing for your clumsiness.

3 Quickly flip the coin under your shoe with your fingertips.

4 Make a fist with your hand, as if you had picked up the coin, and stand up. Then open your hand – and the coin has vanished!

Strike a light!

Things you need

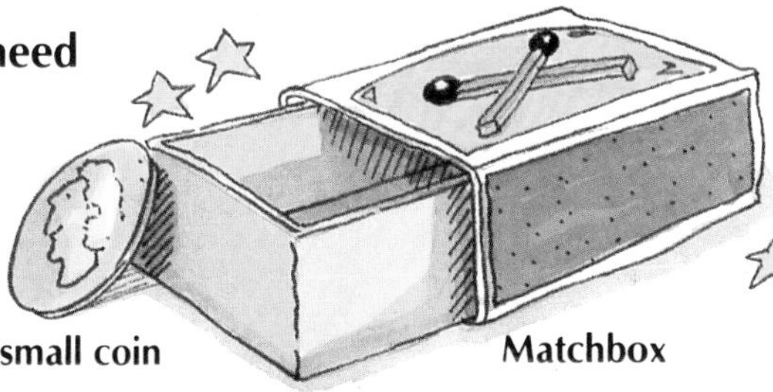
Any small coin
Matchbox

Make a coin disappear from a matchbox.

Trick time

Practise this easy-to-learn trick until it works smoothly.

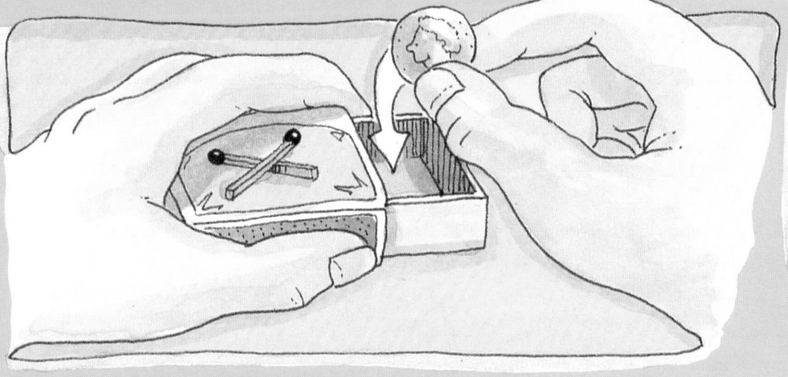

1 Show everyone that the matchbox is empty. Then ask someone to put a coin inside. Close the box and hold it between a finger and thumb, with your palm facing you.

2 Shake the box about so your friends can hear the coin rattling inside.

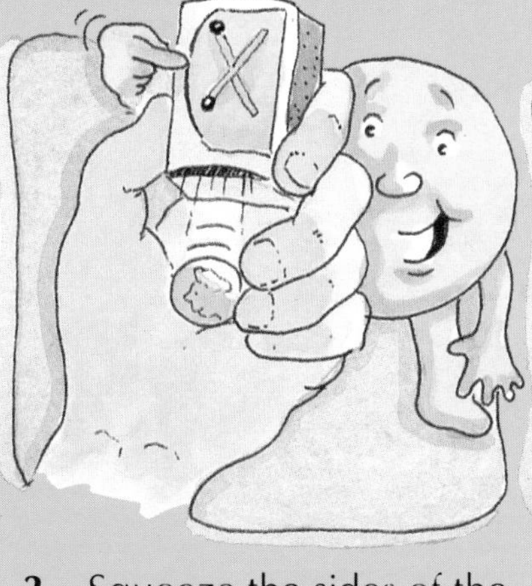

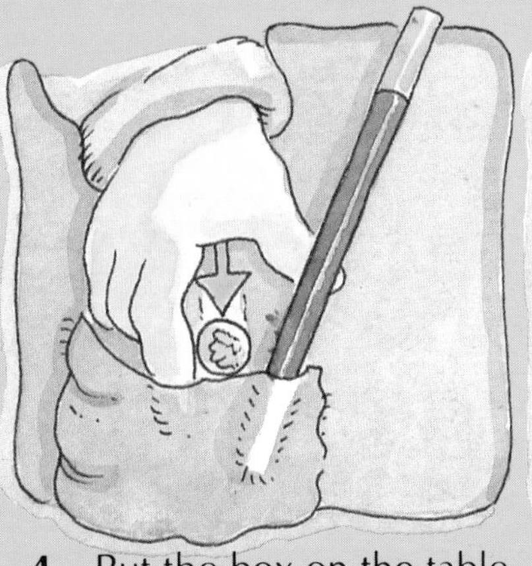

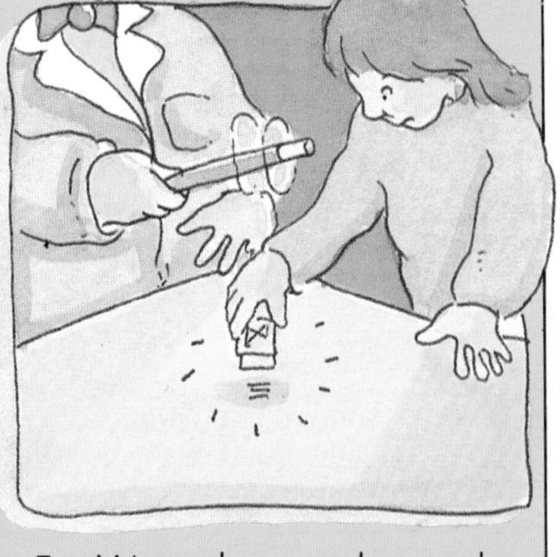

3 Squeeze the sides of the box so the top opens slightly. The coin will drop out into your palm.

4 Put the box on the table. Take the magic wand out of your pocket. At the same time drop the coin in!

5 Wave the wand over the box and ask someone to open it – and it's empty!

Hanky panky

Things you need

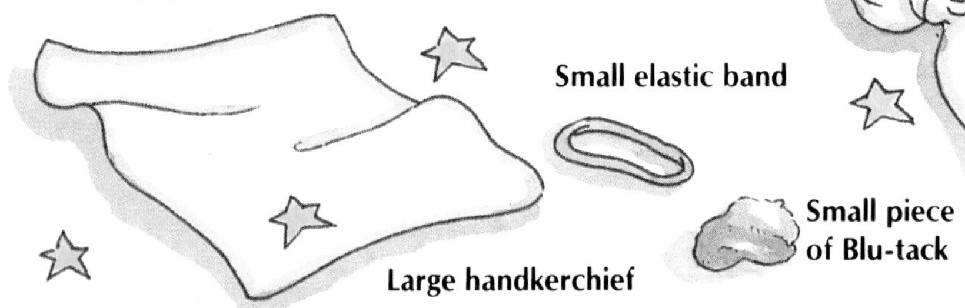

Two easy ways to make a coin disappear under a handkerchief.

Trick time

Hanky panky 1

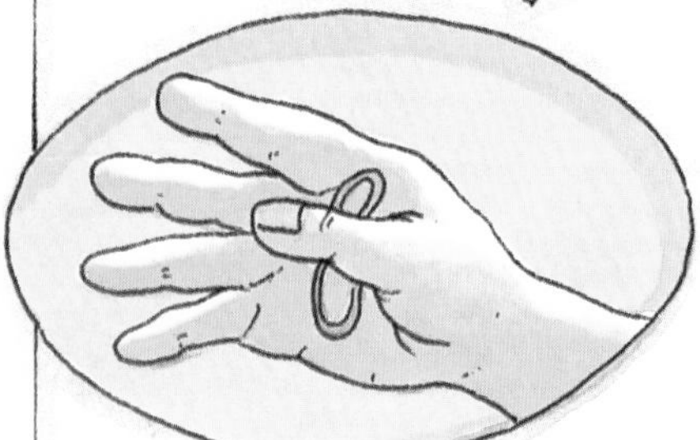

1 Hide the elastic band in your right hand.

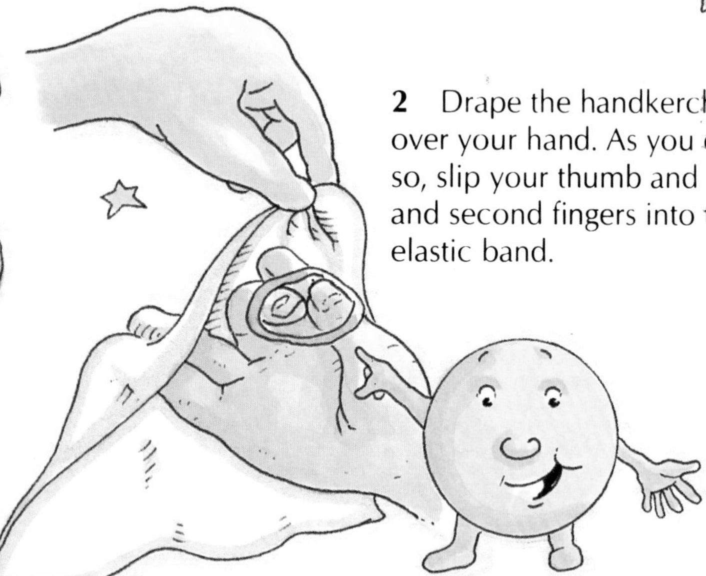

2 Drape the handkerchief over your hand. As you do so, slip your thumb and first and second fingers into the elastic band.

3 Borrow a coin from the audience and push it into the handkerchief. Make sure it goes into the circle made by your fingers stretching the rubber band.

4 Release your thumb and fingers and the elastic band will close, trapping the coin. Now you can shake the handkerchief – and the coin has vanished!

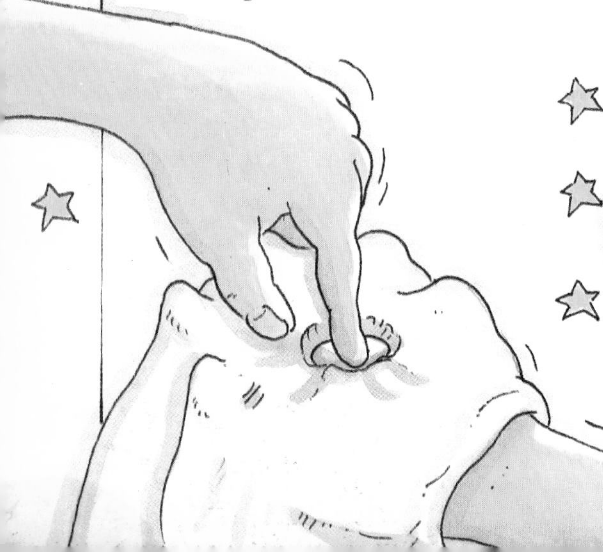

The coin is in this lump at the back!

Hanky panky 2

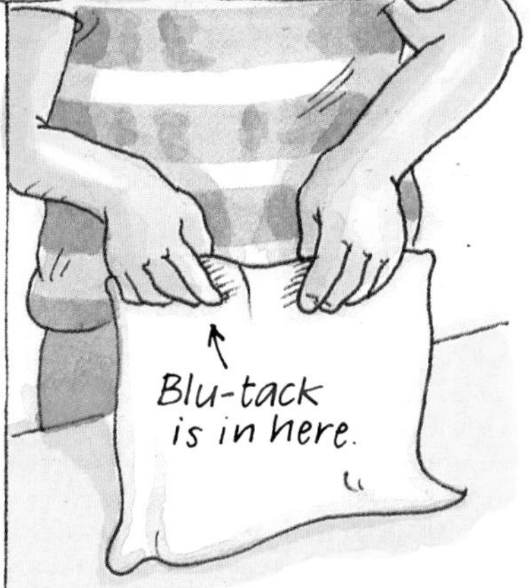
Blu-tack
is in here.

1 Hold the handkerchief out between your hands, with the Blu-tack hidden under your first finger.

Press

2 Lay the handkerchief down on the table, pressing the Blu-tack on to it.

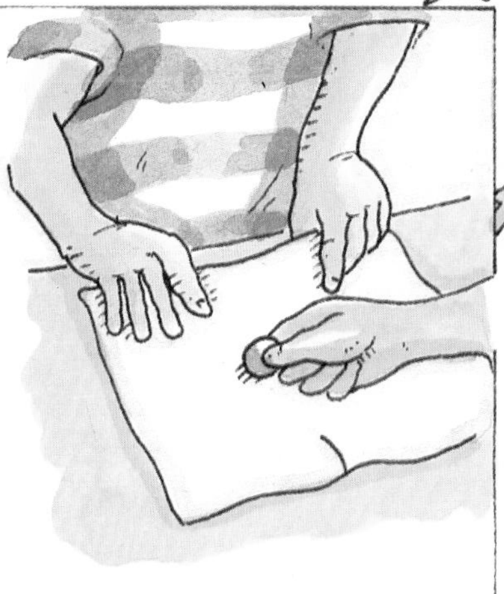

3 Ask someone to put a coin down on to the middle of the handkerchief.

4 Pick up the corner with the Blu-tack on it and fold it over the coin, secretly pressing the Blu-tack down on to it.

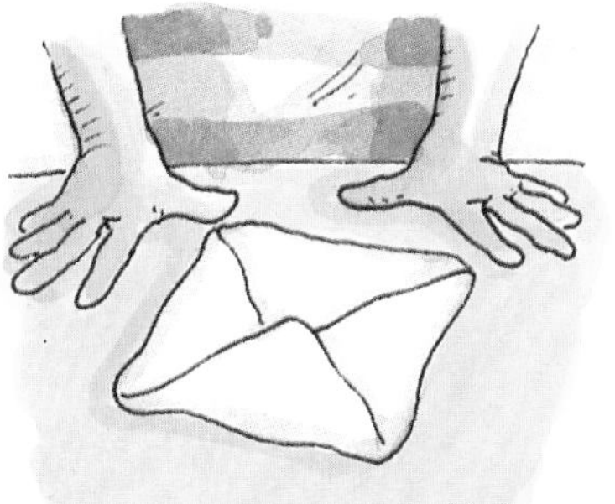

5 Fold the other three corners into the centre.

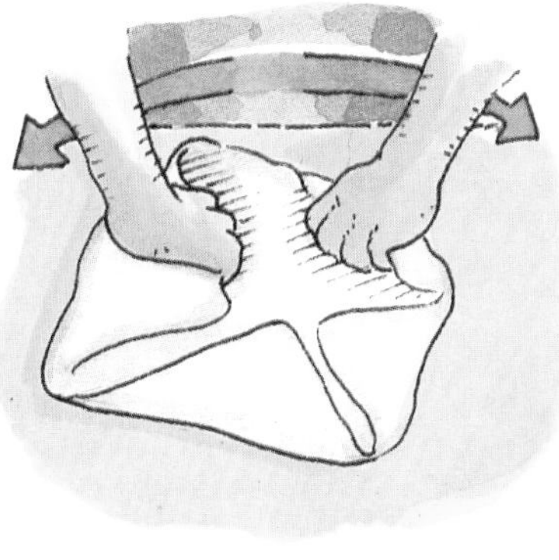

6 Take hold of the edge of the handkerchief and slide your hands apart until they are holding the corners.

The coin is
stuck to the
Blu-tack!

7 Shake the handkerchief – and the coin has vanished!

Cheeky!

Things you need

Handful of coins

Jacket or trousers with pockets

This trick is so simple, you'll need to be really cheeky to get away with it!

Get ready . . .

Start out with the coins in your right pocket. Practise the following moves carefully.

1 Take the coins out of your pocket and hold them in a pile in your right hand.

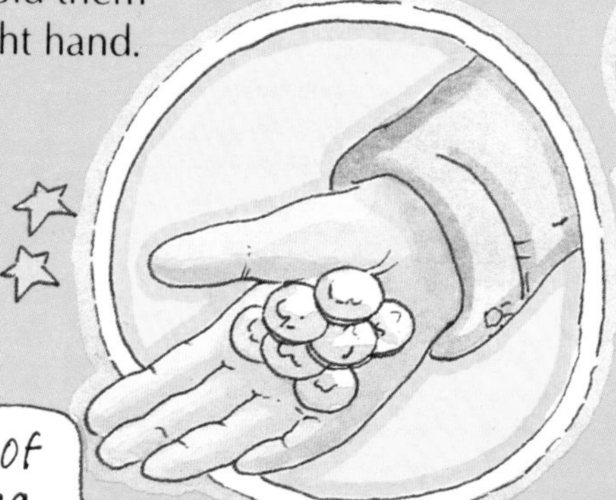

Keep the back of your hand facing towards your audience.

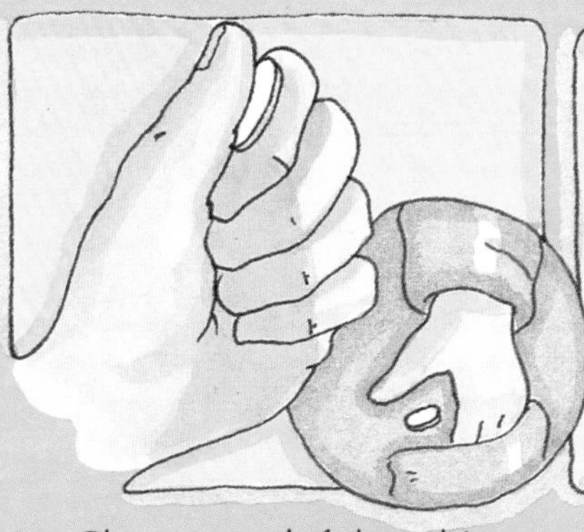

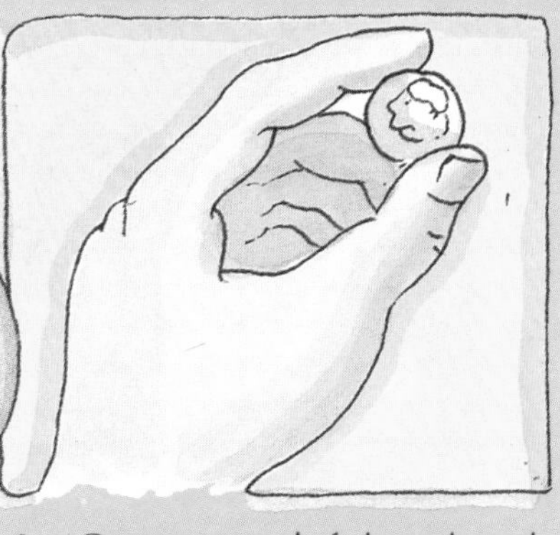

2 Reach across with your left hand and pick out one of the coins.

3 Close your left hand into a fist and **at the same time** put all the other coins back in your pocket.

4 Open your left hand and show the coin.

Practise the four moves shown on the opposite page until you can perform them easily and smoothly. Now you can try the trick.

Trick time

1 When you perform this trick, do all four actions as before – but with one big difference – **don't actually take a coin!**

2 Hold the coins in your hand, as before. But when you get to stage 2, only **pretend** to take a coin.

*So long as everyone **thinks** there's a coin in your left hand, you can make it seem to 'disappear' in any way you like. Why not try inventing your own tricks?*

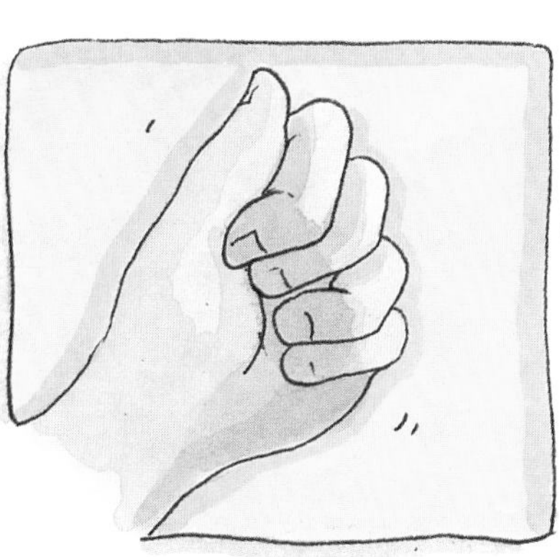

3 Close your fist over an imaginary coin. Behave exactly as you did when there was a coin in it.

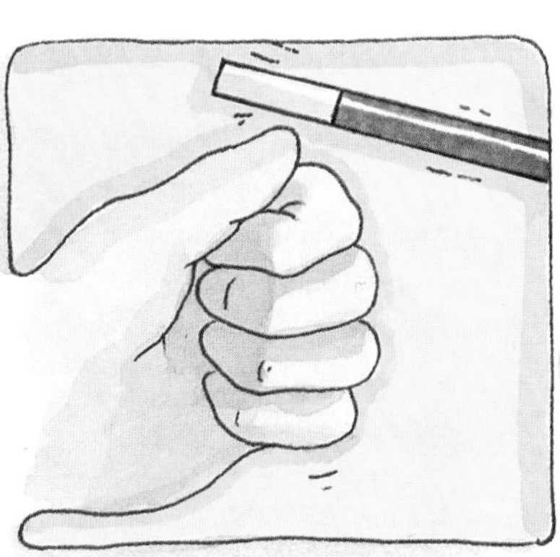

4 At the final stage, tap your left hand with your magic wand. Then open it and show there's nothing there!

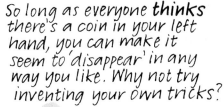

Double your money

Tip six coins into an
empty bag – and take
twelve coins out of it!

Things you need

Twelve small coins, all of the same value

Paper bag

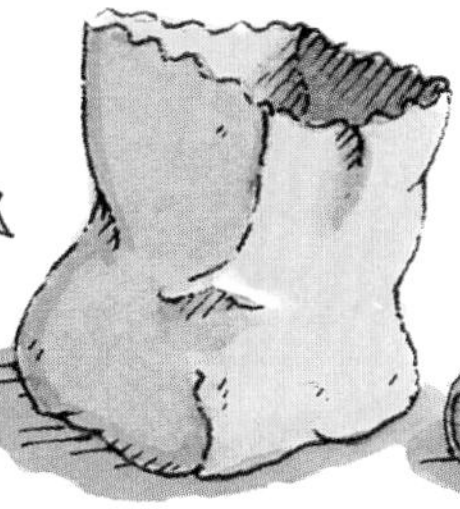

Large hardback dictionary

Get ready . . .

1 Open the dictionary at about the middle. You will now find a gap between the spine and the pages of the book.

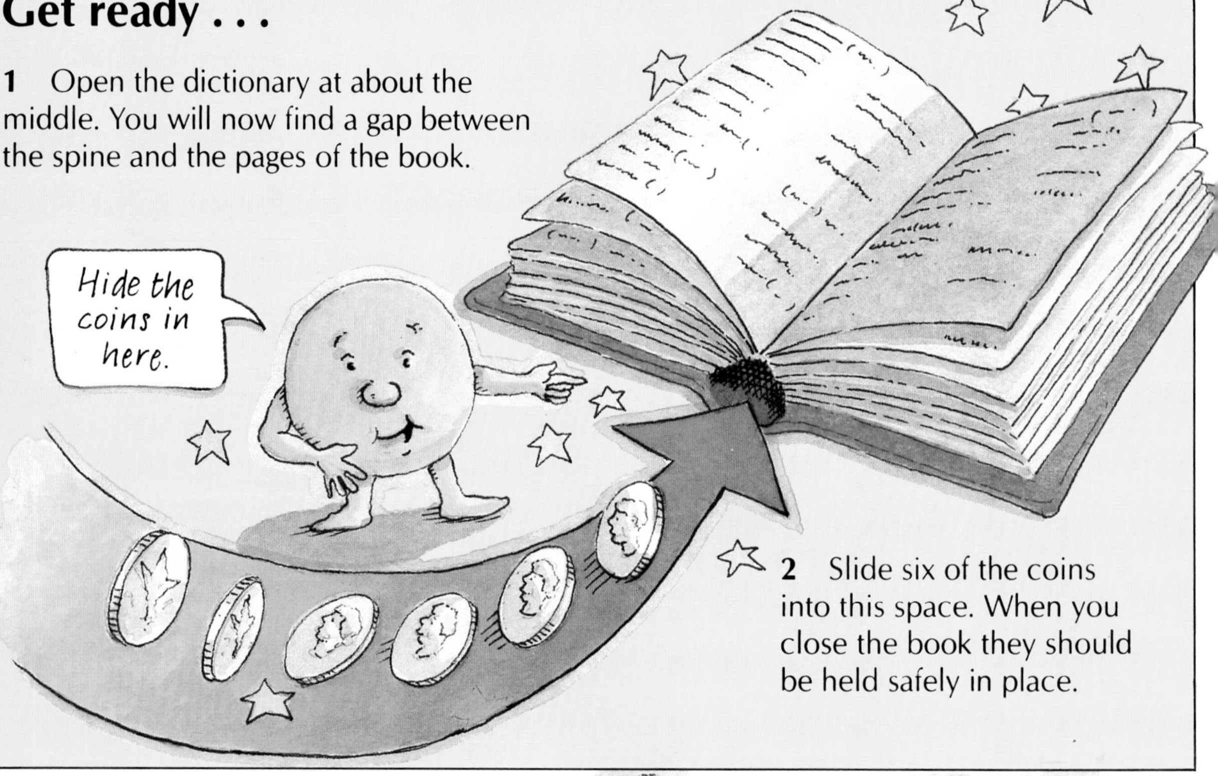

2 Slide six of the coins into this space. When you close the book they should be held safely in place.

Trick time

1 Ask your friends what the word 'magic' means. Say you will check it in your dictionary. Pick up the dictionary, open it near the middle and look for the word 'magic'.

2 Read out the definition and say you will now do some magic by making money double in value!

3 Put the remaining six coins on the open pages of the dictionary and show them to your audience.

4 Open the paper bag, say some magic words, or wave your wand over it, and tip the coins into it.

Of course, the six coins from inside the binding also fall into the bag.

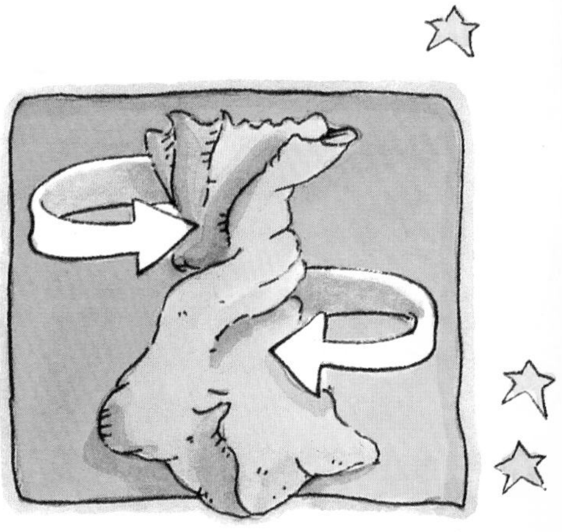

5 Close the bag by twisting the paper round. Give the bag to one of your audience.

6 Ask your friend to open the bag and count the contents. To everyone's surprise the money has doubled in value!

The spooky pencil

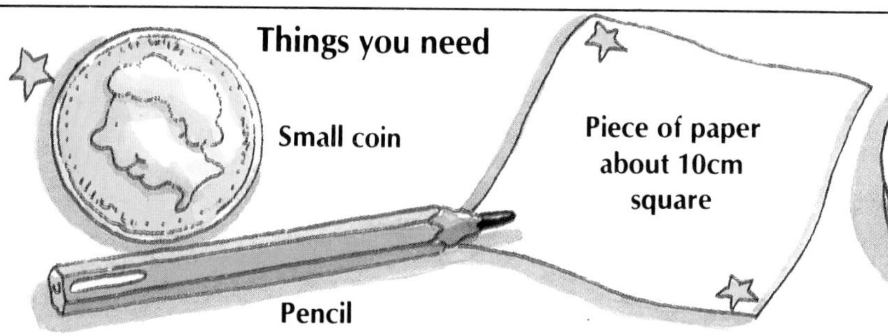

Get ready . . .

Make sure you are wearing something that has pockets. Put the pencil in your right-hand pocket.

Trick time

1 Lay the coin on the paper. Fold the paper as shown in drawings a – d, making a little package.

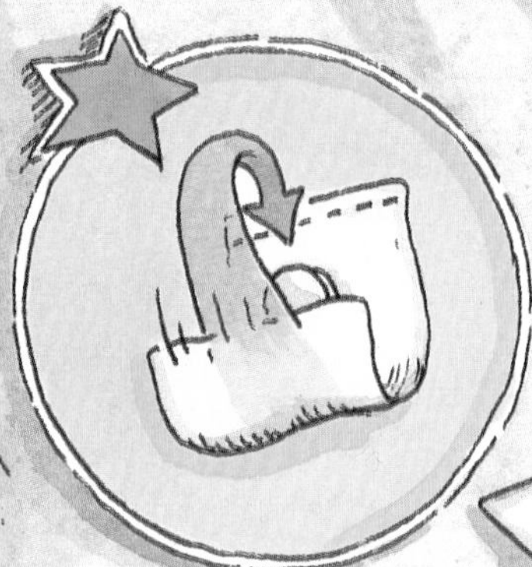

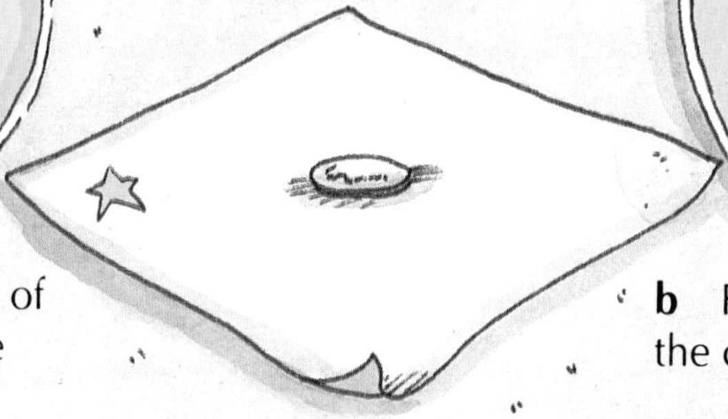

a Fold the bottom edge of the paper up to cover the coin.

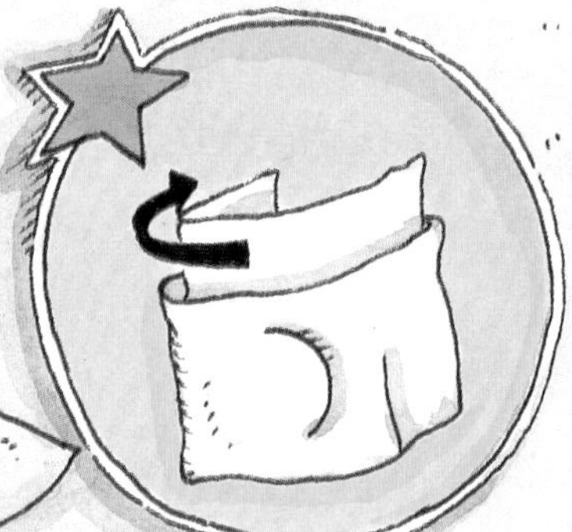

b Fold the left side behind the coin.

Now the coin is in a little package. Only you know it's open at the top.

c Fold the right side behind the coin.

d Fold the flap down behind, *not* over the gap at the top.

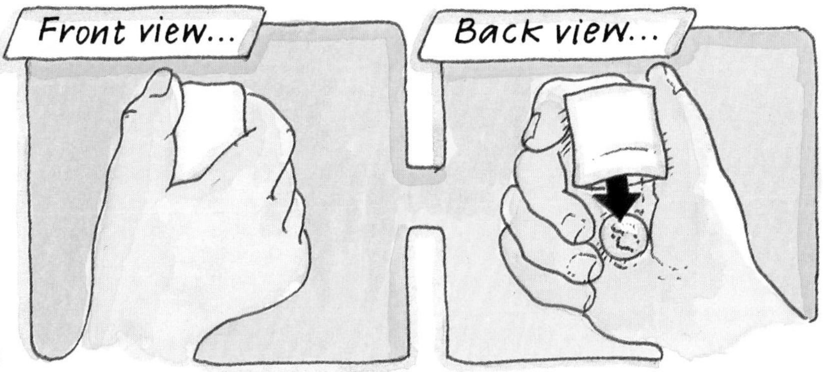

2 Hold the packet in your right hand with the open edge **downwards.** Put your left hand into your left pocket, looking for your pencil.

3 As you do so, squeeze the sides of the packet gently and the coin will fall into your palm.

Drop the coin into your pocket. Then take the pencil out.

4 Of course, you fail to find the pencil in your left pocket. So, transfer the paper packet to your left hand. Put your right hand into your right pocket, taking out the pencil and **dropping the coin in!**

5 Take the paper packet and push the pencil right through it. It looks as if you've pushed it right through the coin!

6 Pass the pencil and paper around for people to examine. Then tear the paper off the pencil – the coin has vanished!

The hypnotized coin

Things you need

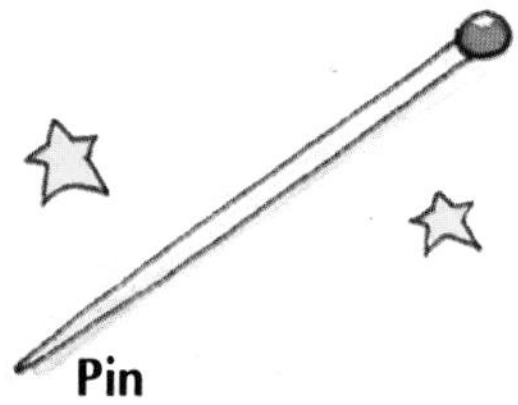

Pin

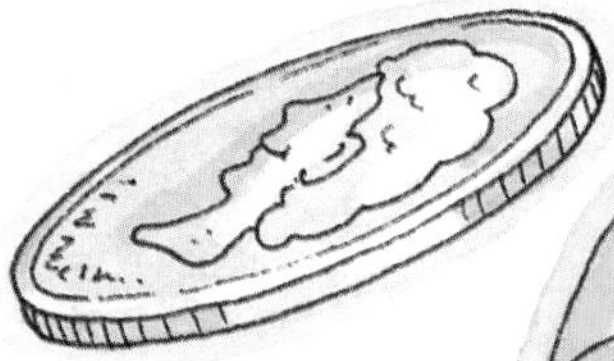

Any large coin

Make a coin move as if hypnotized!

Trick time

The secret is to keep the pin hidden from the audience all the time.

1 Show the coin to your audience, holding the pin behind it so that it is hidden.

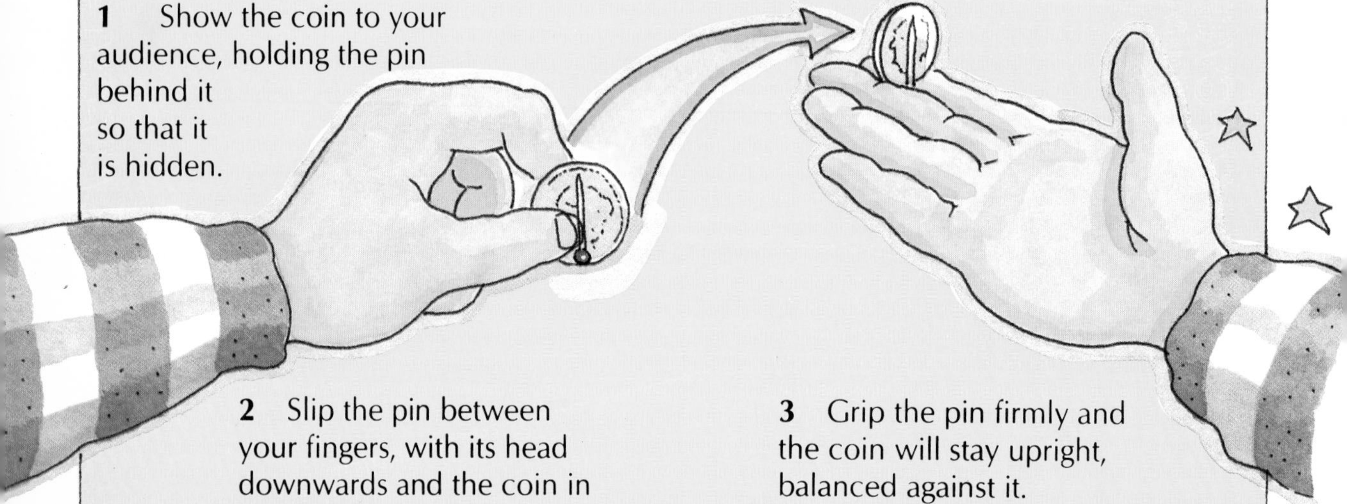

2 Slip the pin between your fingers, with its head downwards and the coin in front of it.

3 Grip the pin firmly and the coin will stay upright, balanced against it.

4 Tell everyone you will now hypnotize the coin. Wave your magic wand, or your hand, over the coin. As you do so, **gradually** release your grip on the pin. The coin will fall slowly backwards on to your fingers, as if hypnotized.

Drop the pin on the floor and nobody will know how you did the trick!

The smashing grab

Trick time

This way of making a coin vanish can be performed on its own or used as part of another trick. Practise your hand movements until they are absolutely smooth and convincing.

If you're left-handed you may find it easier to use the opposite hands.
Slowly open your right hand – and there's nothing in it!
Empty
The coin is in here

1 Hold the coin in your left hand, gripping it between your thumb and first finger. Keep your palm cupped underneath.

2 Move your right hand towards the coin, putting your thumb behind the coin and fingers in front of it. Pretend to grab the coin, but when the fingers of the right hand are hiding it from your audience, **drop it into your left palm.**

3 Go on grabbing with your right hand, closing it into a fist and moving it away as if the coin were inside. Keep your left hand still, with the coin hidden in the palm, held there by the second and third fingers.

Magic elbows

Things you need

Any coin

A shirt, blouse or jacket with a collar

You will also need to be able to do *The smashing grab* trick shown on page 15.

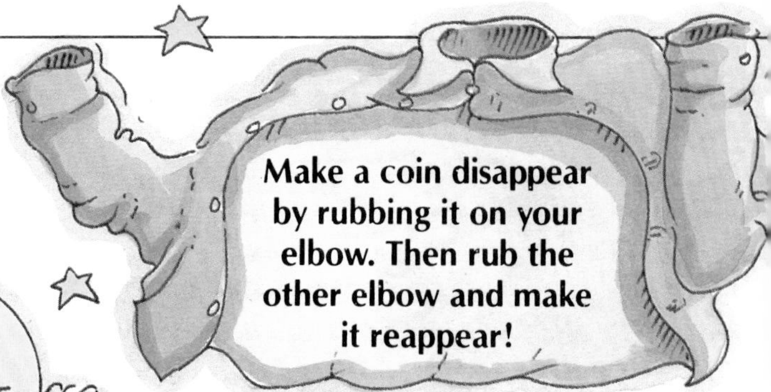

Make a coin disappear by rubbing it on your elbow. Then rub the other elbow and make it reappear!

Trick time

Sit at a table to do this trick.

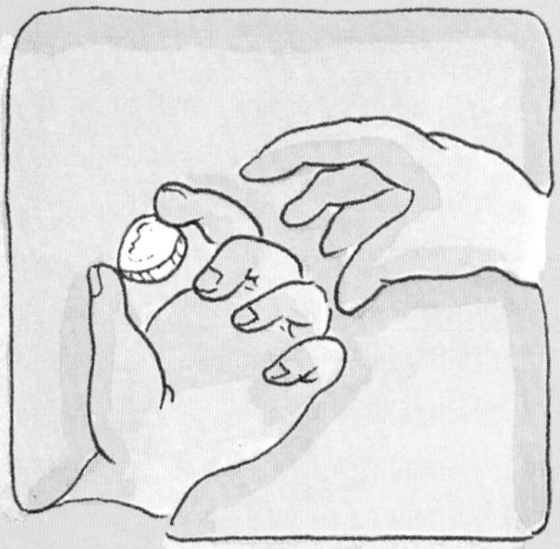

1 Hold the coin in your left hand, as if you were about to do the smashing grab trick (see page 15).

2 Move your right hand towards the coin. Then, instead of **pretending** to take the coin (as in the smashing grab) actually take it in your right hand.

3 Rest your head on your left hand and rub the coin against your left elbow with your fingers.

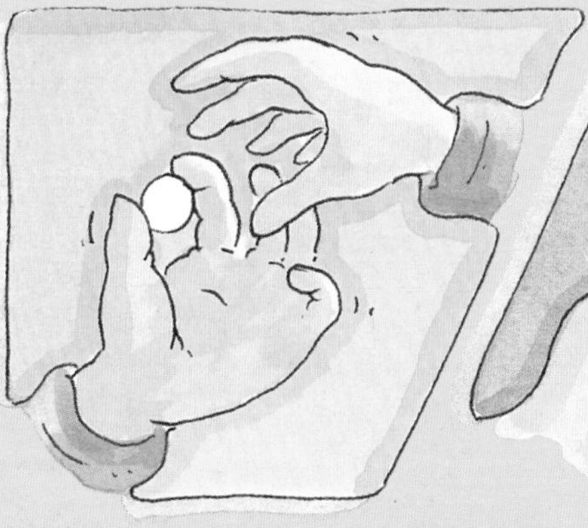

4 Act clumsily and drop the coin on to the table with a clatter. Oh dear, you'd better try again!

5 Take the coin in your left hand as before, but this time do the smashing grab routine properly, so the coin remains hidden in your **left** hand.

Drop the coin into your collar.

6 Lean your head on your left hand and rub your right hand on your elbow, as before. As you do so, drop the coin out of your left hand **inside your collar!**

Tell everyone you'll now make the coin come back.
Take the coin out.

7 After a few seconds, stop rubbing and show there's nothing in your right hand. The coin is rubbed away! Show there's nothing in your left hand, either.

8 Lean your head on your left hand and again rub your left elbow with the other hand. **Grab the coin from your collar and hide it in your left hand.**

9 Rubbing your left elbow doesn't bring the coin back, so lean on the other hand and rub your **right** elbow with your left hand. (Of course, the coin's now in your left hand.) After a few seconds, let the coin fall from your elbow on to the table. Your rubbing has made it come back!

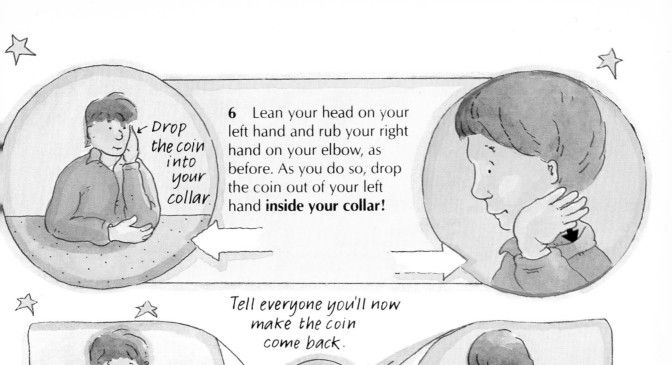

Heads you lose

Things you need

Any coin, preferably large

Make a coin drop out of the sky into your friend's hand!

Trick time

With practice this trick is very convincing - and baffling.

1 Stand facing a friend, holding the coin in one hand. Ask the friend to hold out a hand towards you, palm up.

Say you will count up to three, and when you say "Three" they must try to grab the coin. If they can get it, they can keep it!

2 Raise your hand above your head, then bring the coin down on to their palm.

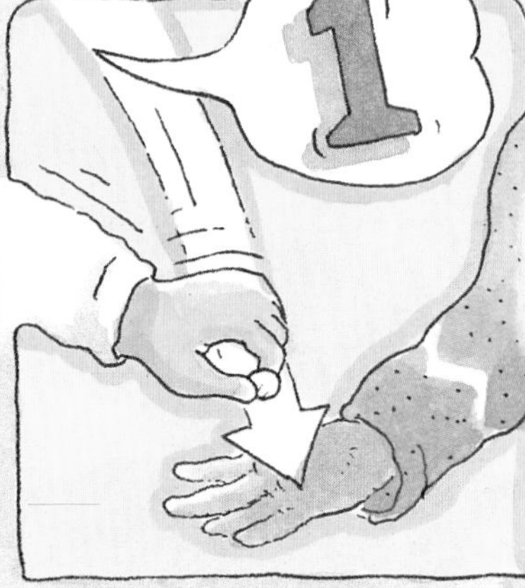

3 As you press your hand into their palm, call out "One!"

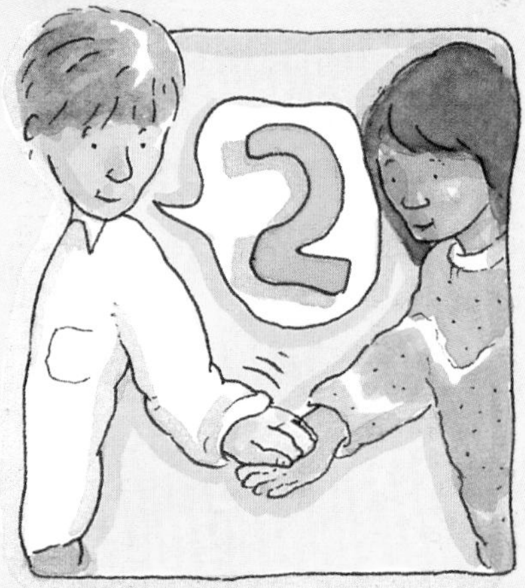

4 Raise your hand above your head again, bring down the coin on to their palm and count "Two!"

5 Raise your hand again, this time placing the coin **on the top of your head!**

6 Lower your hand, press it into their palm and call out "Three!" At the same moment, your friend will make a grab for the coin.

7 Your friend now opens their hand – but there is no coin in it. Open your hand, too, and show the coin has vanished.

8 To make the coin come back, ask the friend to hold their hand out again and stare down at the palm, saying to themselves "Magic money come back!"

Bend over slightly so the coin drops off the top of your head into their hand. Look up to the sky in amazement, as if you can hardly believe it yourself!

Tricky papers

Wrap a coin in three layers of paper - then make it disappear!

Things you need

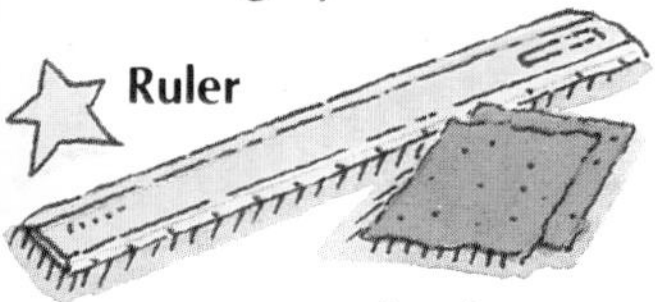

Ruler

2 squares of red paper about 100 x 100mm

2 squares of white paper about 125 x 125mm

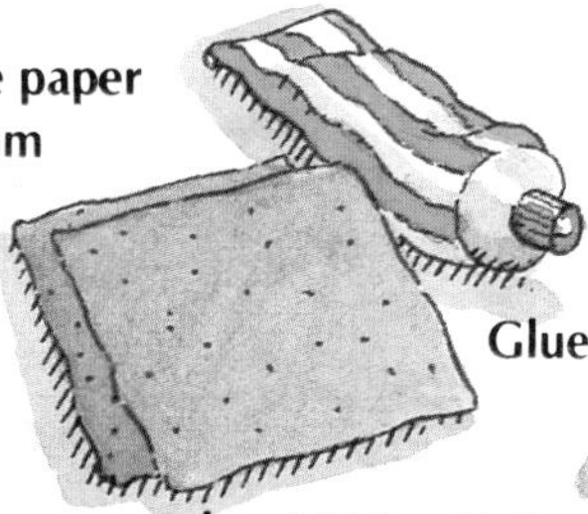

Glue

2 squares of blue paper about 150 x 150mm

Get ready . . .

You first need to make a trick paper packet. Make it as neatly as you can.

You can use paper of any colour, but make sure squares of the same size are the same colour as each other.

1 Take one of the small (red) pieces of paper. Fold about a third of the paper up (33mm).

Fold the top edge down over it.

Now fold the left edge across (about 33mm). Fold the right edge over it, making a square.

You should now have a neat little red parcel about 33mm square.

2 Place the red packet on the centre of one of the pieces of white paper. Fold the white paper around it in the same way to make a packet about 40mm square.

3 Place the white packet on the centre of one of the pieces of blue paper. Fold the blue paper around it in the same way to make a packet about 50mm square.

4 Now make an **identical** set of packets with the other pieces of red, white and blue paper. Make sure they are the same size. **Stick the backs of the blue packets together to make a double packet.**

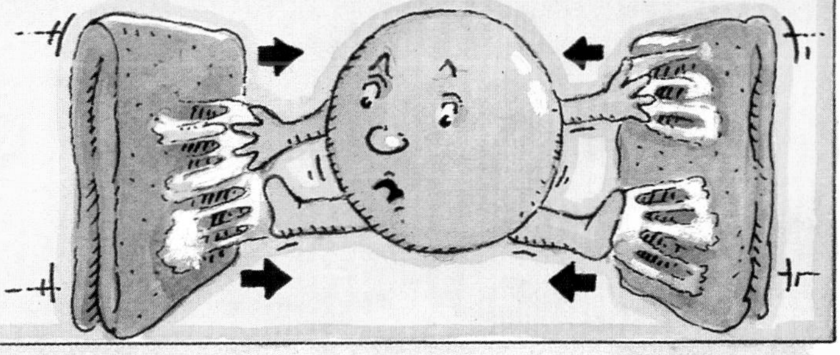

Trick time

1 Place your trick paper packets on the table and open the top set of papers so it looks like this:

2 Borrow a coin from your audience. Put it at the centre of the red paper and fold the red packet up.

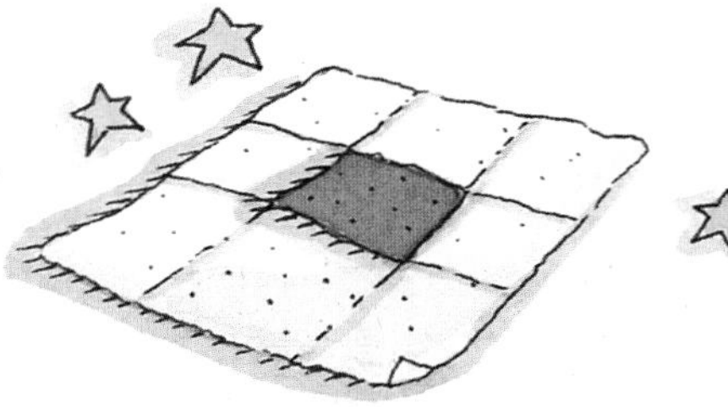

3 Put the red packet on the white paper and fold the sides to make a packet.

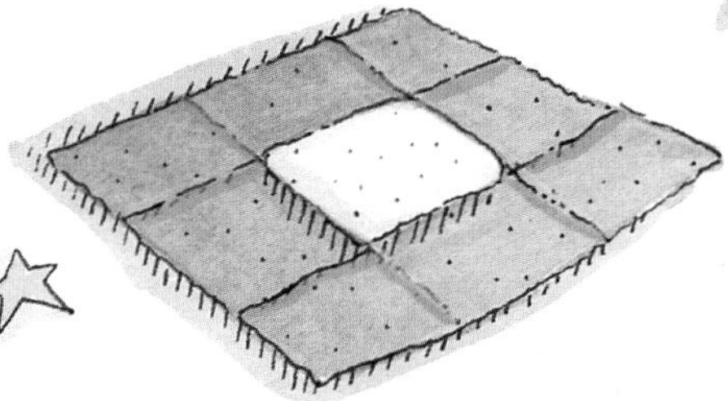

4 Put the white packet on the blue paper and fold the blue paper round it.

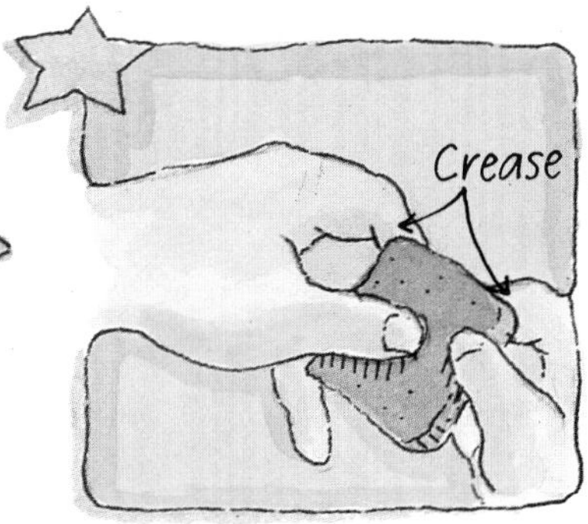
Crease

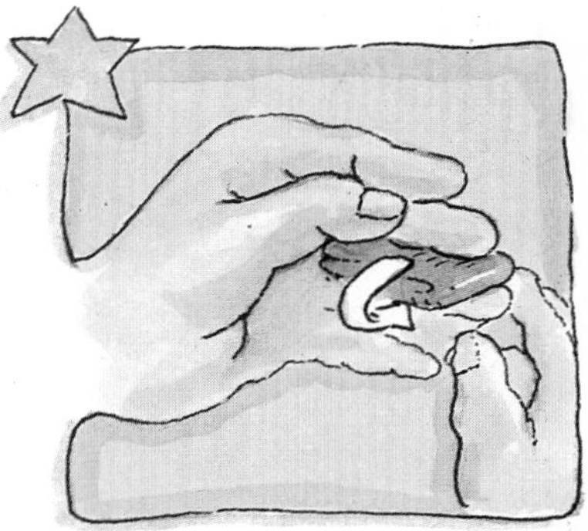

5 Pick up the blue packet when you fold it, carefully creasing the edges. As you do so, **turn the packet over** so the second set of packets (with no coin inside) is on top. Do this casually and nobody will notice.

6 Put the packet back on the table, empty side on top. Wave your magic wand, or your hand, over it. Open the blue packet and take out the white. Then open the white packet and take out the red. Give the red packet to a member of the audience to open.

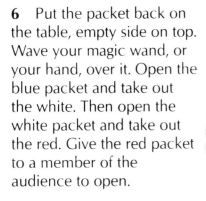

Surprise, surprise! There's nothing in it!

The amazing sealed boxes

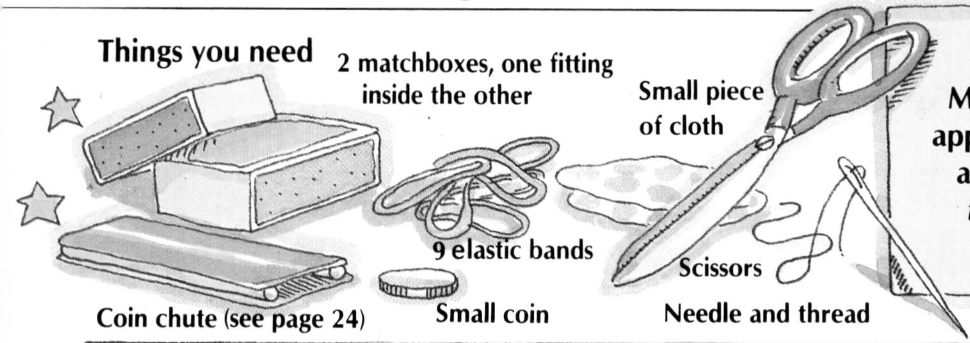
Things you need
2 matchboxes, one fitting inside the other
Small piece of cloth
9 elastic bands
Scissors
Coin chute (see page 24)
Small coin
Needle and thread

Make a marked coin appear by magic inside a sealed bag, inside *two* sealed boxes!

Get ready . . .

1 Fold the cloth and sew it to make a tiny bag. Make sure the end of the coin chute will fit into it.

2 Make sure the equipment is the right size.

3 Put one end of the chute into the cloth bag. Fasten with an elastic band.

Turn the bag inside out.

The end of the chute must fit inside the smaller matchbox.
The small coin must drop easily through the chute.
The small matchbox must fit inside the large one.

4 Put the chute and bag into the small matchbox. Fasten four elastic bands around the box.

5 Put the small matchbox inside the large one, with the chute poking out at one end. Put four elastic bands around the larger box, two in each direction.

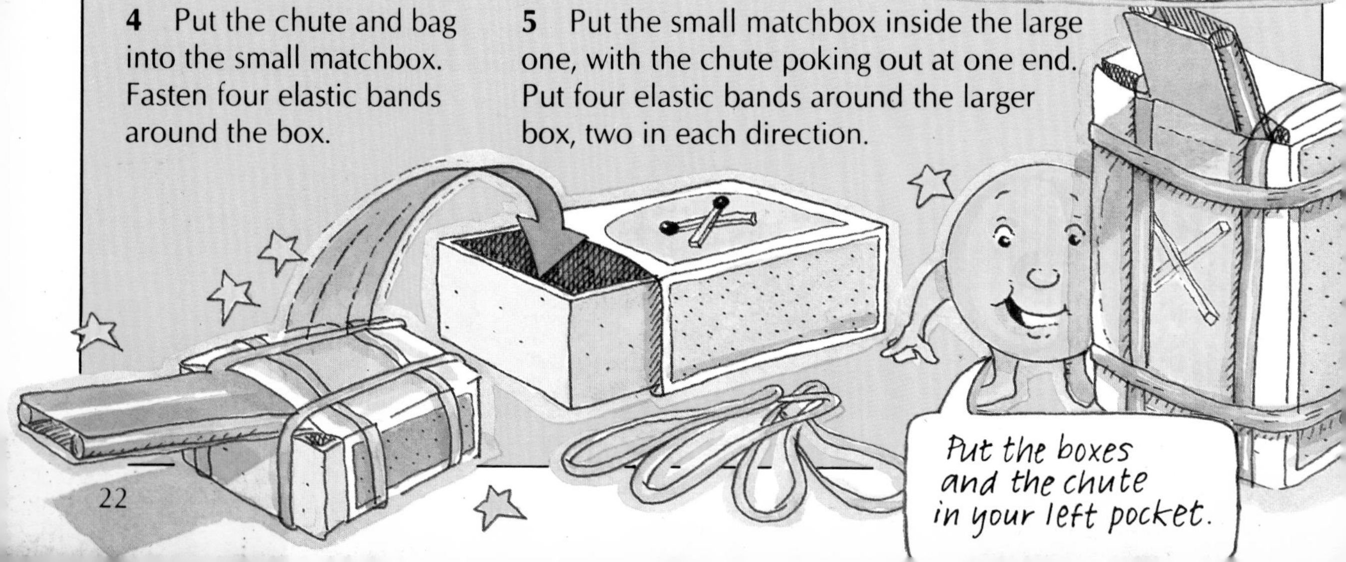
Put the boxes and the chute in your left pocket.

Trick time

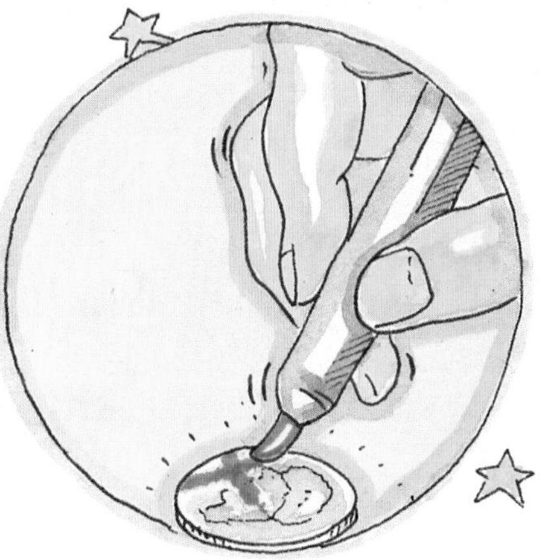

1 Ask the audience for a small coin (of the same size as one you know goes easily through the chute).

2 Ask the person who gives it to you to mark the coin with a pen so they will recognize it again.

3 Do a 'smashing grab' coin vanish (see page 15) so everyone thinks the coin's in your right hand . . . but it's in your *left* hand. Put your left hand into your pocket and drop the coin into the end of the chute.

4 Pull the chute out of the matchboxes. Leave the chute in your pocket and take the boxes out.

5 Give the boxes to a member of the audience. Slowly open your right hand – and the coin has gone!

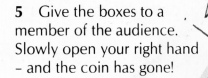

All the elastic bands have tightened, so the boxes are sealed.

That's fantastic!

6 Ask the person to open the sealed matchbox. There's another sealed box inside, with a little bag in it. And inside **that** is the marked coin!

Make a coin chute

Things you need

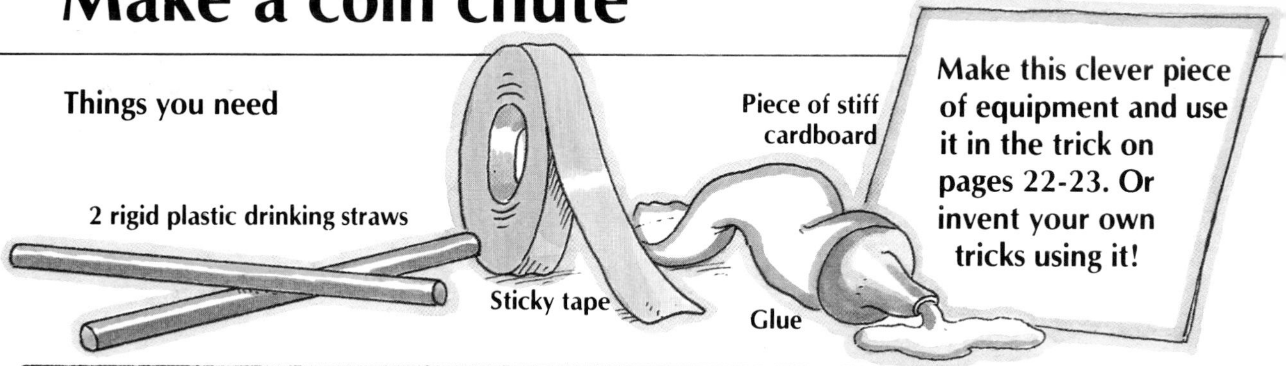

Make this clever piece of equipment and use it in the trick on pages 22-23. Or invent your own tricks using it!

Get ready . . .

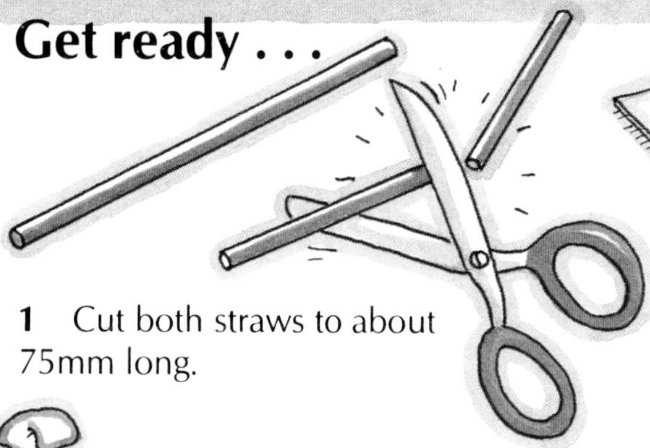

1 Cut both straws to about 75mm long.

2 Cut two pieces of card about 75mm long and about 30mm wide.

3 Glue a straw down each long side of one piece of card. Then glue the other piece of card on top. Now you have a shallow flat tube – a coin chute.

Now try the fantastic trick on page 22!

4 Wrap sticky tape round the chute to hold it firm. Make sure a small coin can drop through it easily.

Produced for Kingfisher Books Ltd
by Times Four Publishing Ltd

Kingfisher Books, Grisewood & Dempsey Ltd,
Elsley House, 24-30 Great Titchfield St, London W1P 7AD

First published in 1991 by Kingfisher Books

10 9 8 7 6 5 4 3 2

Typeset by C-Type, Horley
Colour separations by RCS Graphics Ltd
Printed in Spain

BRITISH LIBRARY CATALOGUING IN PUBLICATION DATA
Day, Jon
Let's make money magic.
1. Conjuring
I. Title II. Fisher, Chris
793.8

ISBN 0-86272-717-0